# TRUCK SONG

BY DIANE SIEBERT
PICTURES BY
BYRON BARTON
THOMAS Y. CROWELL
NEW YORK

Truck Song
Text copyright © 1984 by Diane Siebert
Illustrations copyright © 1984 by Byron Barton
Printed in the U.S.A. All rights reserved.
First Edition

Library of Congress Cataloging in Publication Data
Siebert, Diane.
    Truck song.

    Summary: Rhymed text and illustrations describe
the journey of a transcontinental truck.
    [1. Stories in rhyme.    2. Trucks—Fiction]    I. Barton,
Byron, ill.    II. Title
PZ8.3.S5725Tr  1984        [E]        83-46173
ISBN 0-690-04410-0
ISBN 0-690-04411-9 (lib. bdg.)

country sprawling

lined with roads

trucks are hauling

heavy loads

trucks of metal

trucks of chrome

foot on pedal

far from home

tall trucks

small trucks

parked-for-overhaul trucks

grand trucks

sand trucks

folks who understand trucks:

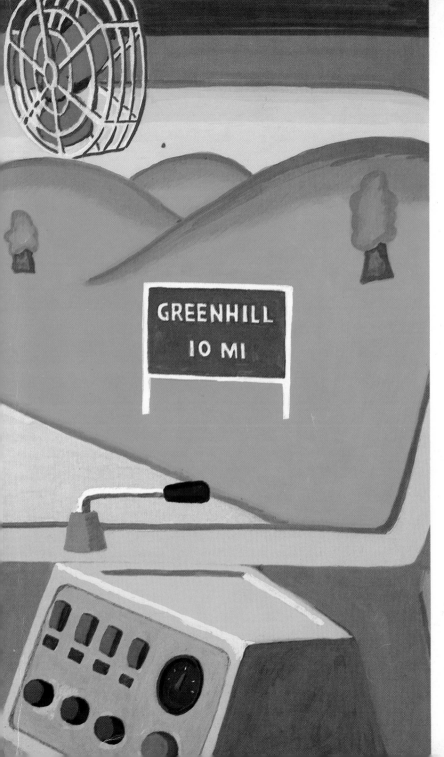

drivers dressed in hats and boots

regulation truckers' suits

crossing interstate frontiers

with eighteen wheels

and

thirteen gears

twin stacks smoke

airhorns blast

brake called "Jake"

to slow down fast

twenty big rigs in a row

down the highway, see them go

giant convoy heading west

"In Dallas, boys, we'll take a rest!"

country music symphonies

truckers talking on CBs

"Thanks, good buddy, big 10–4

I see your rig at my back door!"

white lines

road signs

coffee up ahead

south of town

slowing down

brake lights glowing red

at the truckstop

truckers meet

for road talk

and

a bite to eat

sipping coffee

hot and strong

jukebox plays

a country song

say good-bye

check your load

climb aboard

hit the road

heading out across the plains

checking mirrors, changing lanes

past the farms and fields of wheat

through the rain so cool and sweet

windshield wipers keeping time

lower gear to make the climb

up mountain roads

'round hairpin curves

with eagle eyes

and steely nerves

tractors pull

trailers full

deadlines must be met

journey's end

around the bend

gonna get there yet

off the freeway

into town

shifting

shifting

shifting

down

on every street and thoroughfare

trucks haul goods from here to there

city trucks

pretty trucks

greasy grimy gritty trucks

trucks for moving

trucks for rent

big striped trucks that hold cement

armored trucks that carry cash

garbage trucks that carry trash

tuneful trucks with ice-cream bars

trucks for towing broken cars

trucks

and

more trucks

on the go

through heat

and rain

and sleet

and snow

now up the street and past the light

the loading dock comes into sight

the workers wave as I drive past

I say "Hello!" with one deep blast

then backing slowly to the dock

I sign my papers

check the clock

unload the goods

and when I'm done

I sign up for tomorrow's run

another route

another load—

my rig and I back on the road!